LEWIS AND CLARK
Exploring the Northwest

LEWIS AND CLARK
Exploring the Northwest

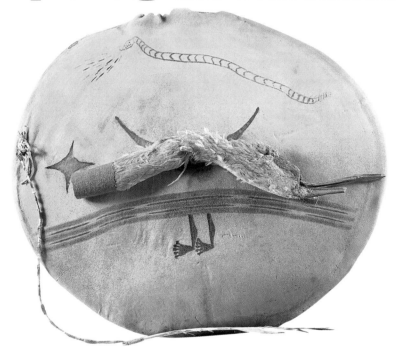

Clint Twist

RSVP

RAINTREE STECK-VAUGHN
PUBLISHERS

The Steck-Vaughn Company

Austin, Texas

Introduction

Meriwether Lewis (left) and William Clark (right), the two leaders of the Corps of Discovery.

Exploration, adventure, and discovery

At the beginning of the 19th century, two young men, Meriwether Lewis and William Clark, set out to explore the western half of America. Their journey to the Pacific Ocean and back took them about 4,350 miles. They traveled through territory that had never before been explored by white people. Most of the trip was made by river, often in small canoes. The rest of the time they traveled on horseback, or struggled along on foot.

The journey was full of hardships and adventure. Lewis and Clark encountered Native American warriors, fierce grizzly bears, and poisonous snakes. They crossed dusty deserts, climbed snow-covered mountains, and braved fierce river rapids. They built their own boats, hunted their own food, and made log forts for protection. It was also a journey full of discovery and wonder. They made friends with the Native Americans that they met and learned much about their different cultures. They also discovered many new species of plants and animals. Best of all, they were able to make the first accurate maps of the American West.

The rugged scenery of the Rocky Mountains. Lewis and Clark crossed these mountains on foot and on horseback.

Seventy years after Lewis and Clark made their historic journey, trains such as this were taking passengers across the American West.

Horizons

After reading this book, you may want to find out more about the journey of Lewis and Clark. Or you may become interested in a particular place or topic. At the end of some of the chapters, you will find **Horizons** boxes. These boxes list the names of people, places, and objects that are not mentioned in this book, but that are a part of the story of America. By looking these up in the indexes of other reference books, you will discover more about the times in which Lewis and Clark lived.

An official expedition

Lewis and Clark did not travel alone. They were the joint leaders of an official expedition of some 30 to 40 explorers who were known as the Corps of Discovery. The expedition was organized and paid for by the American government. All of the members of the Corps of Discovery were government employees.

In 1800, the United States was a young country, and it was much smaller than it is today. However, it was growing quickly. Lewis and Clark's historic journey began a process that was to continue throughout the 19th century. Encouraged by the American government, settlers were to move steadily westward. At the beginning of the century, the Corps of Discovery had to travel by canoe, on horseback, and on foot. By the end of the century, it was possible for ordinary people to travel all the way from the Atlantic coast to the Pacific coast by train.

Detailed records

Acting on the instructions of the American president, Lewis and Clark kept careful records (or journals) of their journey. Besides writing down the distance and direction they traveled each day, they also described in detail the people and places they saw.

The journals of Lewis and Clark provide the modern reader with a fascinating glimpse into American history. They describe a world that has long since passed, as well as telling the story of an amazing feat of exploration. Just as Columbus opened up a "New World" for Europe, so Lewis and Clark helped to open up the American West for the United States.

The Historical Background

The *Mayflower,* in which Pilgrim settlers from England sailed to America in 1620.

An illustrated map showing French settlers arriving at Port Royal in eastern Canada, in 1605.

Europe and America

At the end of the 15th century, Christopher Columbus discovered a continent previously unknown to Europeans: America. Most of the newly discovered land in America was claimed by Spain, the country that had paid for Columbus's voyage, although the eastern portion of South America (Brazil) was granted to Portugal. Stories of gold and treasure brought thousands of European settlers to America. The Portuguese settled in Brazil and the Spanish in Mexico, Bolivia, and Peru. Although some Spaniards settled in Florida, they did not venture much farther into North America. The people who settled in North America came mainly from three other European nations: France, England, and the Netherlands.

Patterns of settlement

The English settled along the eastern coast of North America. The first permanent English colony was founded at Jamestown, Virginia, in 1607. In 1620, a group of religious exiles called the Pilgrims left England in a ship named the *Mayflower*. The Pilgrims established a colony far to the north of Virginia at Plymouth, Massachusetts.

The French settled along the St. Lawrence River in what is now Canada. They established colonies at Quebec and Montreal and gradually expanded southward. French explorers sailed down the Mississippi River in 1673, and five years later they reached the Gulf of Mexico. The French claimed all the territory along the Mississippi from Canada as far as the Gulf of Mexico. They named this vast territory Louisiana.

The Dutch settled at the mouth of the Hudson River. In 1626, they bought the island of Manhattan, where they built the town of New Amsterdam. However, they lost their colony to the English in 1664, and New Amsterdam was renamed New York.

By the end of the 17th century, the eastern half of North America had been divided between France and England, although the Spanish still held on to Florida. But the claims of England and France clashed, and the American colonies

New Amsterdam, the capital of Dutch America, pictured in the early 1650s before it was taken over by the British, who renamed it New York.

became involved in wars between the two European powers.

Between 1689 and 1763, four wars were fought in North America between France and England. Americans and Canadians became involved as settlers were recruited to join the fighting. Native American tribes also fought on both sides. In 1707, England united with Scotland to form the new nation of Britain. At the end of the wars, it was the British who were triumphant. At the final peace conference in 1763, France lost most of its North American territory. Britain was given control of Canada and Florida, and Louisiana was given to Spain.

British America

After 1763, Britain ruled virtually all the settled areas of North America. By this time Britain's 13 colonies in North America stretched along the East Coast from Massachusetts in the north to Georgia (named after the British king) in the south (see map on page 8). The colonists elected their own local assemblies, but they were not allowed to send representatives to the British

White settlers dressed as Native Americans throw cases of imported tea overboard during the Boston Tea Party.

Parliament in London. Another cause of discontent was that the British government would not let settlers move west of the Appalachian Mountains. However, the colonists' main complaint was about the taxes that they had to pay to the British government on imported goods. The colonists objected to the British government taking money from them when they had no representatives in the British Parliament.

In 1773, a group of colonists dressed as Native Americans staged a protest by throwing a cargo of imported tea into the harbor at Boston. This event became known as the "Boston Tea Party," and was an early indication of American dissatisfaction with British rule.

Americans in revolt

In 1774, representatives of 12 of the 13 colonies met at the First Continental Congress in Philadelphia. Among other things, the representatives decided to stop trading with Britain. This was an act of open defiance. In April of the following year, the first clash between British soldiers and American colonists took place at Lexington, Massachusetts. This was the first armed encounter in the American War of Independence.

The American colonists had no trained army, no navy, and very little money. Against them stood the most powerful navy in the world and a well-equipped and experienced army. Despite this, the colonists were determined to fight. The Second Continental Congress met in May 1775, and George Washington was

The Original 13 Colonies

The 13 colonies that became the original United States were New Hampshire, Massachusetts, Connecticut, Rhode Island, New York, Pennsylvania, New Jersey, Delaware, Maryland, Virginia, North Carolina, South Carolina, and Georgia. The flag of the new United States, the first "Stars and Stripes," had 13 stars and 13 stripes (one for each state). Additional stars have since been added as new states have joined the union.

1 Massachusetts
2 New Hampshire
3 Rhode Island
4 Connecticut
5 New York
6 Pennsylvania
7 New Jersey
8 Maryland
9 Delaware
10 Virginia
11 North Carolina
12 South Carolina
13 Georgia

The Original 13 Colonies

A painting showing the members of the Continental Congress signing the Declaration of Independence (above).

George Washington, soldier and statesman, who defeated the British in the Revolutionary War and later became the first President of the U.S.

appointed the Commander in Chief of the newly created American army.

The outbreak of war convinced many of the colonists that the only answer was a complete break with Britain. On July 4, 1776, Congress voted to adopt the Declaration of Independence. In the future, the 13 colonies were to be independent states.

The Americans were given support by some other European countries, especially France. Finally, in 1781, an American and French army surrounded the British at Yorktown, Virginia. The British army surrendered. In effect, the war was over, but a final peace treaty was not signed until 1783.

The American states were now an independent nation, the United States of America. In 1787, representatives of all the states except Rhode Island met in Philadelphia to draft a constitution for the country. This constitution was ratified by the states in 1788 and became the law of the land. George Washington was elected the republic's first President in 1789.

The United States of America

In addition to recognizing the independence of the 13 states, Britain also handed over a huge area of land between the Appalachian Mountains and the Mississippi River. Although it was relatively large in area when compared to some European countries, the United States had only a small population. The first census (population count) taken in 1790 showed that there were just under four million Americans. Of these, about half a million were black slaves living mainly in the southern states. There were only five cities with a population of more than 10,000. Most Americans lived on farms or in small towns, and there was hardly any industry. Most manufactured goods were imported from Europe.

By the middle of the 1780s, settlers had already established themselves to the west of the Appalachians. New roads were built connecting towns and cities throughout the growing country, and new states were carved out of these western lands. Kentucky became a state in 1792 and Tennessee in 1796. Ohio, Indiana, Illinois, Michigan, and Wisconsin followed over the next 60 years.

New Orleans in 1841. Farm products from the American West were shipped from New Orleans to the eastern coast of North America and to Europe.

The United States began to change in other ways. Although primarily an agricultural nation, industry and trade began to develop, especially in the Northeast. Cotton had been an important crop in the South for almost 100 years. Then in 1790, Samuel Slater opened the first cotton-spinning factory in Pawtucket, Rhode Island. The manufacture of cotton cloth rapidly became an important industry in New England.

As the nation developed its western lands, farmers in these areas began shipping potatoes, fruit, flour, and other products down the tributary rivers of the Mississippi River. The Ohio, Illinois, and Tennessee rivers became great trade highways. Once the products reached the Mississippi River they were shipped south to the port of New Orleans. From here the farm products of the West were sent to markets along the eastern coast of North America and to Europe. New Orleans was the all-important gateway for the growing agricultural wealth of the United States, and in 1800 the port of New Orleans belonged to France.

The French Revolution

France had been the strongest ally of the United States during the American Revolution. In 1789, one year after the United States adopted the Constitution, France underwent its own revolution. The people of France overthrew their king and set up a republic. Some European nations opposed the revolution and declared war on France.

The elected government of France did not last very long. A young soldier named Napoleon Bonaparte seized power and reorganized the government. Between 1799 and 1802, Napoleon defeated most of the other European nations, including Spain. As a result, the French got back Louisiana, which had been given to Spain in 1762. New Orleans was part of Louisiana.

Napoleon Bonaparte, pictured in 1800 when he was at the height of his power.

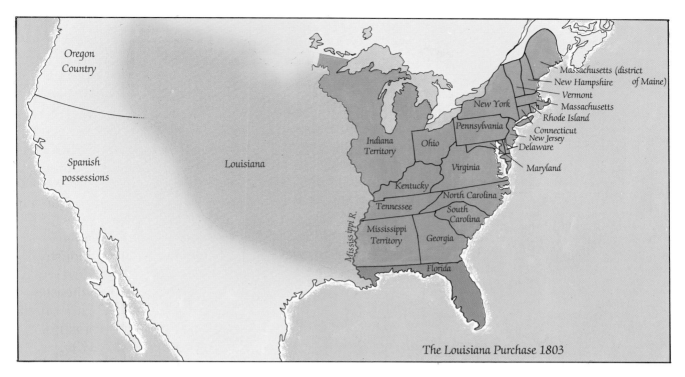

The Louisiana Purchase 1803

The Louisiana Purchase

Thomas Jefferson was elected President of the United States in 1800. He was deeply concerned about the transfer of New Orleans to the French. New Orleans was vital to the economy of the United States, and Jefferson did not want to see the port closed to American trade. In 1802, Jefferson gave the American representative in France orders to purchase New Orleans and West Florida from France, if possible. A sum of $2 million was offered. In response, the French asked how much the United States would pay for all of Louisiana. The United States finally offered $15 million for the whole territory, and the offer was accepted.

The purchase of Louisiana was one of the biggest bargains in American history. Although no one knew the exact size of Louisiana, the purchase at least doubled the size of the United States. Having made the purchase, the American government wanted to know exactly what it had bought. The only information about Louisiana came from trappers who roamed great distances in search of beaver, bear, and mink. There were few facts, a great many stories, and no accurate maps. In order to find out more about what was now called the Louisiana Territory, Thomas Jefferson arranged for an expedition to be made along the Missouri River to explore the territory. The expedition was to collect scientific information, and try to find a land and river route to the Pacific Ocean. The men chosen to lead the expedition were Meriwether Lewis and William Clark.

Horizons

You could find out about these people who all lived about the same time as Lewis and Clark: Paul Revere (a hero of the American Revolution); Lafayette (a French officer who fought in both the American and French revolutions); Dr. Joseph Guillotin (inventor of a beheading machine that became the symbol of the French Revolution); Duke of Wellington (British general who defeated Napoleon); Andrew Jackson (seventh President of the United States and the first from a state west of the Appalachian Mountains).

Preparing the Corps of Discovery

Thomas Jefferson, who sent Lewis and Clark on their journey.

A vision of the future

Thomas Jefferson was born in Virginia in 1743. In 1800, he was elected the third President of the United States. Jefferson was an experienced politician, and had been a member of the Continental Congress during the War of Independence. Later he had served as ambassador to France, and as a secretary of state. Jefferson was in favor of expanding the United States westward, and was one of the first American politicians to urge settlers to move toward the Mississippi River. The chance to buy Louisiana and the important Mississippi River port of New Orleans fit perfectly with his vision of America's future. During the months of discussion that led to the purchase, Jefferson wrote: "The future destinies of our country hang on the event of this negotiation."

In 1803, the negotiations were completed successfully, and the United States bought the whole of Louisiana. The Louisiana Territory stretched westward from the Mississippi River, but how far was not known exactly. It certainly did not stretch as far as the Pacific coast because the lands on the western coast of North America had already been claimed by other nations. In the south, the Spanish owned California. To the north of California was the Oregon Territory, which was an extension of British Canada.

The boundaries between these western territories were extremely vague, and the region had never been properly explored by anyone except Native Americans. Jefferson organized the first official exploration party to find out exactly what lay west of the Mississippi River.

A portrait of Meriwether Lewis painted just after the return of the expedition. He is wearing a fur shawl that was given to him by the Shoshone tribe.

Expedition leadership

Jefferson chose an army officer, Meriwether Lewis, to lead the expedition. Like the President, Lewis was from Virginia, and he had been Jefferson's private secretary until 1803. The two men got along well together. Jefferson trusted Lewis to carry out his instructions to the letter.

At the time he was made expedition leader, Lewis was 28 years old. He was young and fit, he was an experienced soldier, and he had the skills of a diplomat. Jefferson knew that the success of the expedition depended on establishing good relations with the local Native Americans. In order to make sure that Lewis was fully

A page from Clark's journals. Lewis and Clark made detailed descriptions and drawings of the plants and animals they saw on their journey.

Clark's journal, bound in elkskin for protection.

prepared, the President sent him to Philadelphia where he studied Native American culture.

The choice of co-leader was left to Lewis. He approached another Virginian, William Clark, who was an old friend from the army. Clark was a few years older than Lewis, and had considerable experience dealing with Native Americans. Lewis and Clark made a good team. Lewis was generally quiet and thoughtful, while Clark was more outgoing and optimistic.

President Jefferson expected a lot more from the expedition than simply the discovery of a route to the Pacific. He wanted to know everything possible about the Louisiana Territory and what lay beyond. Lewis and Clark were to draw detailed maps of every part of the expedition's route, and to pay special attention to features such as waterfalls and rapids, which would affect the passage of boats. They were to take careful observations of the sun and stars, so that they could work out their exact position in terms of latitude and longitude. They were also to keep detailed records of the weather, noting what the cloud cover was, and recording the temperature, and on how many days it rained.

In fact, the expedition was to take note of everything it came across. The soils were to be assessed for fertility, and any mineral deposits were to be described in detail. If any new plants or animals were discovered, specimens were to be collected and brought back to the United States. Jefferson was so concerned about this that he instructed Lewis to study botany and zoology in addition to Native American culture.

President Jefferson was particularly interested in the Native American inhabitants of the region. He wanted to know what the various tribes were called, where they lived, and how they were organized. Lewis was given strict instructions to be friendly at all times, and to inquire about possibilities for trade.

The most important instruction that the President gave the expedition was also the simplest — write it down! Jefferson knew that it was no use taking detailed measurements and collecting information if good records were not kept. He told Lewis to make extra copies of every report that he wrote, and even suggested writing one copy on birch bark because it was more waterproof than paper.

The Corps of Discovery

Lewis and Clark agreed that about half the members of the expedition should be experienced soldiers, while the rest should be recruited from people who lived near the Missouri River. One of the most useful recruits was George Drouillard, the son of a French Canadian father and a Native American mother. Drouillard was an expert in the sign language that some of the tribes used to communicate with strangers, and he became the expedition's chief hunter and interpreter.

Lewis organized the men into a formal Corps of Discovery, which had its own rules and regulations. Those who broke the rules would be thrown out of the Corps immediately, and could be left behind to make their own way back to the United States. The founding members of the Corps of Discovery were Lewis and Clark (both with the rank of captain), three sergeants, about 40 men with the rank of private, and Clark's black servant who was named York.

At the end of 1803, the Corps of Discovery made camp at the mouth of the Wood River (then known by the French name Dubois), near the village of St. Louis. During the winter they prepared for the expedition.

Riverboats

The most important task during the winter of 1803-04 was the construction of the boats in which the Discoverers (as they sometimes called themselves) would start the journey upriver. They built three boats: a keelboat and two smaller pirogues.

Today, St. Louis is a large modern city. The soaring archway symbolizes the city's position as gateway to the American West.

Drawing of a keelboat similar to the one that carried the Corps of Discovery up the Missouri River.

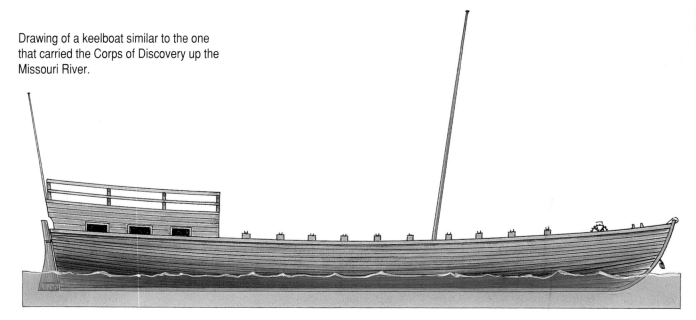

The keelboat was a flat-bottomed boat about 52 feet long. The design was based on the box-shaped barges that were often used to carry cargo. Steering was by means of a single rudder at the stern. Pointed ends and a keel running along the bottom also made the boat easier to steer. The keelboat was designed for shallow water and could float in a depth of just less than 3 feet. At the back of the boat, there was a small raised deck, with a few cabins beneath. Most of the crew traveled on the open deck, sheltered by a canvas roof.

When traveling downstream, a keelboat was carried along by the flow of the river. However, the Corps of Discovery intended to travel upstream, and that meant moving against the flow of the water. When the wind was in the right direction (blowing upstream), the Discoverers could hoist the sails. But most of the time, the keelboat had to be rowed or poled along by human muscle power. When progress became very difficult, the keelboat could be towed with ropes from the riverbank.

The word *pirogue* is taken from the name used by native Caribbean islanders for their dugout canoes. The word came to North America with French and Spanish settlers and was used

The Arrival of Steam

Lewis and Clark's expedition came at the end of the time when ships and boats had to rely only on wind or muscle power to move. At the same time as the Corps of Discovery was exploring the Missouri River, the American engineer Robert Fulton (1765-1815) was designing the first practical steamboat.

The steam engine had been perfected during the 18th century by the Scottish engineer James Watt (1736-1819). By 1800, steam engines were becoming widely used as pumps in mines and for powering machinery in the first European factories. During the 19th century, engineers such as Robert Fulton developed ships powered by steam engines.

In 1807, Fulton's steamboat, the *Clermont*, began the world's first steam-powered shipping service along the Hudson River between New York and Albany. In 1811, just five years after Lewis and Clark's return, another Fulton-designed steamboat, the *New*

Orleans, made the first steam voyage up the Mississippi River. Within a few years, Mississippi steamboats driven by paddle wheels were to become a familiar sight, carrying passengers and cargo up and down the river. The first steamboat service on the Missouri River started in 1819, and by the 1830s there were about a dozen boats in operation on the river.

A Mississippi steamboat in 1879. Paddle wheels on either side of the ship pushed it forward.

to refer to any small boat designed for shallow water. Pirogues were especially popular with hunters in the swamps and marshes along the Mississippi River, where a good pirogue was said to be able to "float on dew." The pirogues used by the Corps of Discovery could each carry about ten people. They had rainproof canvas covers that could also be used as sails, but most of the time they too were rowed or poled upriver.

The Native Americans also made dugout canoes, some of which were elaborately carved. But they preferred lightweight canoes made out of a thin outer covering stretched over a curved wooden framework. In the far north, birch bark was widely used for the outer covering because it was waterproof, and could be sewn like material. Elsewhere, animal hides were used to cover the framework.

A Native American canoe, made from animal hide stretched over a carved wooden framework.

The camp chest that Clark took with him on the expedition.

Lewis knew that the keelboat and pirogues would probably have to be abandoned at some point, so he prepared for this in advance. He designed an iron framework for a canoe some 30 feet long, which was made and packed into crates. When it was needed, the framework was to be unpacked, put together, and covered with animal skins, so that the expedition could continue upriver. But when this collapsible boat was finally assembled and launched, it would not float. Lewis had forgotten to include some pitch for waterproofing the seams, and there were no pine trees in the area from which to obtain waterproof resin. Instead the expedition made dugout canoes.

Supplies and equipment

Although Lewis forgot the pitch for the collapsible boat, he was in fact a very careful organizer. He made detailed lists of everything the expedition would need:

A ship's chronometer
(accurate clock) (top) and sextant
(below), similar to those used by Lewis
and Clark.

Food Lewis and Clark planned that the expedition should feed itself from the wild, surviving mainly on meat from hunted animals or food obtained by trade with the Native Americans. For emergencies, the expedition took 50 barrels of preserved pork, 550 pounds of dry biscuits, 192 pounds of dried soup, and over 26 gallons of brandy.

Weapons Although the members of the expedition wanted to establish friendly relations with the Native Americans, they had to be prepared for anything to happen. All the explorers were armed with rifles or muskets, and the officers had pistols. The keelboat also had two small cannons on swivel mounts.

Scientific equipment In order to take the detailed measurements required by President Jefferson, Lewis packed a full set of surveying equipment, including measuring chains, a spirit level, a quadrant, a sextant, and several compasses. He also took an accurate clock, known as a chronometer.

Medicine chest Both Lewis and Clark had some medical knowledge, and the expedition carried a well-equipped medicine chest containing more than 20 remedies.

Presents In terms of cost, gifts were the biggest single item on Lewis's list. Altogether, more than 50 different kinds of presents were taken including axes, knives, scissors, mirrors, magnifying glasses, thimbles, beads, ribbons, blankets, rings, earrings, brooches, needles, fishhooks, and wire, together with some special gifts for the Native American chiefs.

All of these supplies, as well as many other tools and items of camping equipment such as tents, spare clothing, and cooking utensils, were packed into 21 great bales and 2 boxes. These were somehow stowed aboard the 3 boats without sinking them.

Guns

Each member of the expedition carried a flintlock rifle or musket. One member of the expedition, John Shields, was a gunsmith. He kept all of these weapons in working order throughout the journey. Afterward, Clark said that the expedition owed much of its success to this fact.

However, relying on guns sometimes could be risky. When one member of the expedition got lost, he nearly starved to death, even though there were plenty of wild animals around. He had a gun and gunpowder, but no lead balls. In the end, he managed to survive by shooting a rabbit using a piece of wood instead of a lead ball. The journals note with amazement how the lack of a small lead ball nearly cost a man his life.

A muzzle-loading rifle

Across America — the Journey of Lewis and Clark

On Monday, May 14, 1804, William Clark led the Corps of Discovery out of its Wood River camp and began the journey up the Missouri River. Meriwether Lewis was delayed in St. Louis by last-minute official business, and did not join the expedition until a few days later. On May 21, under the joint command of Lewis and Clark, the expedition continued upstream. Within a week the Discoverers had traveled beyond the last white settlements on the river and entered unsettled territory.

The men soon became skilled at handling the keelboat and pirogues, and the expedition made steady progress through a wooded landscape. By the end of June, the explorers had reached the site of present-day Kansas City. Soon afterward, they passed through a stretch of forest that had been devastated by a tornado. Trees with trunks more than 3 feet across had been snapped in two like matchsticks. Violent weather was not the only hazard that the explorers faced. Lewis noted several times in his journals that the mosquitoes were "very troublesome."

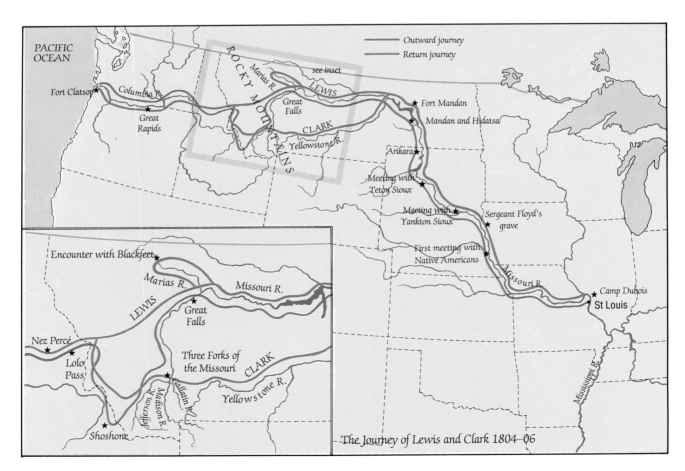

The Journey of Lewis and Clark 1804–06

Lewis and Clark meet with Native Americans. This picture was drawn by Patrick Gass, a member of the expedition.

First encounters

At the beginning of August, the expedition made its first contact with some Native Americans. A messenger was sent out to invite the local chiefs to a meeting by the river. Six chiefs of the Oto and Missouri tribes arrived, and their names were recorded. Lewis made a long speech explaining the purpose of the expedition. Each chief made a speech in reply, and presents were exchanged. The Native Americans and the explorers then shared a meal together, and parted on friendly terms.

Bison, often called buffalo, once roamed the plains in huge numbers.

Continuing upriver, the expedition sailed past a large sandbar that was completely covered with thousands of nesting pelicans. These birds spent the winter in Florida and on the Gulf Coast, but came inland to breed during the summer. Farther upstream, Lewis collected some samples of minerals that he found by the riverbank. To try to find out what they were, he tasted them and nearly poisoned himself.

At the end of August, the expedition made contact with members of the Yankton branch of the Sioux nation, and a formal meeting was arranged. Clark was able to learn a great deal about the Sioux, and he made a vocabulary of their language.

As they continued their journey, the explorers found themselves traveling through open grassland with only a few trees. This was the beginning of "buffalo country," the huge rolling prairies grazed by vast herds of bison. However, Lewis was much more interested in the prairie dogs (small rodents), which made their homes in underground burrows. To him, prairie dogs were a completely new species of animal.

At the end of September, the expedition came upon villages occupied by the Teton branch of the Sioux. The Teton Sioux were not friendly toward the explorers and tried to prevent them from leaving their campsite. After a few tense moments, a Teton chief calmed his warriors and allowed the expedition's boats to leave peacefully. In October, the expedition passed into the territory occupied by the Arikara tribe and established friendly relations with these Native Americans. At the end of October, the explorers arrived at the villages of the Mandan and Hidatsa tribes and decided to make a winter camp because the river would soon be covered in ice.

Pictured by Patrick Gass, members of the expedition build a fort for the winter.

The first winter

The Mandan were a distant branch of the Sioux nation and lived a fairly settled existence in villages. Lewis and Clark directed the construction of a sturdy log fort near the Mandan villages in which to wait out the winter.

The winter of 1804-05 was a very cold one in the far north of the Louisiana Territory. On January 10, 1805, Clark's thermometer recorded a temperature of -40° F. Each day, two or three men would go out hunting; otherwise, the members of the expedition stayed inside their log cabins. When the weather got a bit warmer, it was possible to venture outside for longer periods. Clark recorded his own activities on a typical

Mandan hunters perform the buffalo dance to make their next hunt successful.

Charbonneau and Sacagawea

Toussaint Charbonneau was a French Canadian trader who had been living among the Mandan for some time. He was married to a Native American woman named Sacagawea, and they had an infant son named Jean Baptiste. Sacagawea was not of the Mandan tribe; she was a Shoshone, and had been kidnapped when she was a young girl.

Sacagawea turned out to be an even more important recruit than her husband. Her local knowledge was invaluable, and even during the most severe hardships, she showed a steadfast determination and courage.

Sacagawea had valuable knowledge of local Native Americans.

winter's day. First, he helped Lewis to make astronomical observations of a lunar eclipse. Then he supervised the men in an unsuccessful attempt to chip the boats out of the ice. Finally he amputated the toes of a Native American boy who was suffering from frostbite. All in a day's work for an explorer!

Toward the middle of March, the expedition prepared to leave. The boats were freed from the ice, and Lewis hired a new interpreter named Toussaint Charbonneau and his wife, Sacagawea. The expedition leaders had decided that the keelboat could not travel any farther upriver, so they sent it back to St. Louis. With it went all the specimens and samples that had been obtained so far, as well as Lewis and Clark's journals. Several members of the expedition went back with the keelboat as crew while the rest continued their journey in the two pirogues and six canoes. At the beginning of April 1805, the Corps of Discovery began its journey up the Missouri River again.

The Great Plains

Gradually, the course of the river curved around until the expedition was traveling almost directly westward. Up to this point Lewis and Clark had been fairly sure of their route because of reports brought back by hunters. Now they were moving into the unknown. In his diary, Lewis compared himself to Columbus and Captain Cook, traveling by boat where no white man had been before.

There was certainly a lot to discover. On the plains there were many species of wildlife that were new to Lewis, including gophers and the American avocet. The expedition also came across grizzly bears for the first time, and soon learned to treat these fierce animals with respect. One man was chased up a tree by a wounded grizzly. He was forced to stay there for three hours until the bear wandered away.

The grizzly bear is the largest and fiercest carnivore (meat-eater) in America.

Members of the expedition above the Great
Falls of the Missouri River.

The Great Falls

At the beginning of June, the expedition reached
the mouth of a river that Lewis named the
Marias River, after his cousin Maria Wood. In
order to lighten their load for the journey ahead,
the explorers decided to bury a cache. The men
dug a large hole and buried one of the pirogues
together with all the supplies and equipment
that they could manage without. They intended
to recover the cache on their return journey.

On June 13, they arrived at the Great Falls of
the Missouri River. This magnificent waterfall
was measured by Clark who found it to be over
820 feet wide and nearly 98 feet high. The
explorers made camp while they considered
how to go around the falls. They constructed
wooden carts so that they could push their
canoes and baggage overland. However, they
were forced to travel a distance of 18 miles to
skirt the falls, and it took nearly a month of
exhausting work to get the entire load to the
other side. Here, Lewis intended to use his
collapsible iron boat, but this experiment
proved to be a failure (see page 16). Instead
the explorers made new dugout canoes in which to continue
their journey.

The Three Forks

At the end of July, the explorers came to the Three Forks in
today's Montana where three rivers flow together into the
Missouri. Lewis named the rivers Jefferson, Madison, and Gallatin
in honor of the President and two other important Americans. As
they followed the Jefferson River toward the mountains, Lewis

The Continental Divide

The Continental Divide is the name given to
the watershed that separates westward and
eastward flowing waters in North America.
In the United States, the Continental Divide
follows the line of the Rocky Mountains. On
August 12, 1805, Lewis traced the source of
the Missouri River to a small spring gushing
from the eastern slope of a small ridge. On
the other side of the ridge, he drank water
from a stream that ran westward. This stream
eventually ran into the Columbia River. By
walking over the ridge, the party had crossed
over the Continental Divide.

Rising up from the North American Great Plains are the
mountains that form the Continental Divide.

and Clark began to take turns going ahead with an advance group, while the rest of the expedition followed.

After ten more days of travel, the advance party (with Lewis in charge) reached a point where the Jefferson River became too shallow and narrow to continue by canoe. Lewis left a message for the others and set out on foot. A day or so later Lewis saw what he had been looking for — a Native American on horseback. Very cautiously he approached, but the horseman took fright and rode off. Lewis was disappointed because he needed to obtain horses from the Native Americans in order to continue on the next stage of the journey. When Lewis eventually managed to establish contact with the Native Americans, they were identified as Shoshone. Several of the Shoshone accompanied Lewis back to where Clark was waiting with the rest of the party. Here a happy surprise awaited, as the local chief turned out to be the brother of Sacagawea (see page 21), and the helpful cooperation of the Shoshone was now assured.

Across the mountains

After Lewis and Clark had explained the purpose of their expedition, the Shoshone chief made them a sand map showing them what he knew of the region's geography. According to the map, they had to go over many mountains before they would reach a river that would take them to a "great shining lake" (the Pacific Ocean). Lewis obtained horses from the Shoshone to carry their supplies. The Shoshone warned the explorers that they would have to take all their food with them, because there were few wild animals in the mountains.

The explorers set out at the end of August, climbing through rugged country as the weather turned colder. By the middle of September, they were above the snowline and traveling through coniferous forests. They crossed the mountains at the Lolo Pass and began to descend. Food supplies were now running low, and Clark went on ahead with a group of six men in order to search for something to eat. After a few days, they arrived at a Native American settlement and sent back for Lewis and the rest of the party.

The Native Americans on the western slopes of the mountains belonged to the Nez Percé tribe. They lived in villages near the banks of the Clearwater River. The Nez Percé chiefs told Lewis and Clark that they could reach the sea by traveling down the river. Heartened by this news, the explorers built themselves new dugout canoes. At the end of September, they left their horses with the Nez Percé for safekeeping and set off down the river.

Traveling with the flow of the river, they made good progress, and by mid-October they reached territory inhabited by the Yakima tribe. Although they did not stop long, Lewis noted how the Yakima caught the salmon that migrated up the river once a year. The salmon were hung on poles and dried, to provide food throughout the winter.

At the end of October, the expedition passed through the Great Rapids of the Columbia River, and entered the territory of the Chinook nation. Among the Chinook, Lewis and Clark noticed far more manufactured items than they had seen since leaving the Mandan. This was because the Chinook traded with white people from the Pacific Coast.

Pacific winter

Toward the end of their journey, the explorers sometimes covered more than 30 miles in a day. Finally, on November 7, 1805, they sailed into the tidal waters at the mouth of the

A modern replica of Fort Clatsop where the corps spent the winter of 1805-06.

Columbia River. They had finally arrived at the Pacific Ocean.

After two weeks of exploration, Lewis and Clark decided to build a winter camp. They held a vote among the corps to choose the best site. They called this camp Fort Clatsop, after the name of the local branch of the Chinook nation. Fort Clatsop was built of logs. It was a square shape, with each side measuring about 52 feet.

There was little to do during the winter. Lewis and Clark spent most of the time writing an account of their journey. Clark drew a map of their entire route, with the positions of the rivers carefully marked according to the survey measurements that they had taken. The two men also gathered a considerable amount of information about the coastal trade between white people and the Native Americans, and made a list of the names of the ships that visited regularly.

Homeward bound

When spring came, the explorers began to prepare their canoes for the return journey, and on March 23, 1806, the Corps of Discovery started back upriver. A month later, the explorers abandoned their canoes and recovered their horses in order to continue overland. Once again they crossed the mountains through the Lolo Pass.

After the hardships of the mountain crossing, the explorers rested for a few days. When they did set out again at the beginning of July, it was as two separate parties. Lewis and six men took a direct eastward route toward the Missouri. Clark and the rest first headed south and then turned east. The two groups arranged to meet where the Yellowstone River flows into the Missouri.

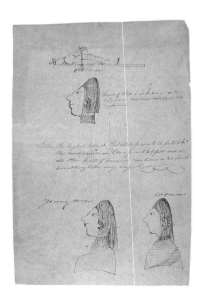

Clark made sketches of the Native Americans that lived near Fort Clatsop. These people had their foreheads flattened when they were infants, using the device shown at the top.

Lewis's group traveled overland to the Missouri and then to the Marias River. One evening, they were approached by a small hunting party from the Blackfoot tribe. Early the next morning, the Blackfeet tried to steal some guns and horses. There was a fight, and two Native Americans were killed. This unfortunate incident was the only outbreak of violence between the white

Clark led most of the corps back along the Yellowstone River.

Horizons

You could find out about the following places in the United States that are also associated with the journey of Lewis and Clark: the Gates of the Mountains (in Montana); Lemhi Pass (site of the Continental Divide on the Montana-Idaho border); Mount Adams (in Washington State); Lewis and Clark Lake (on the Nebraska-South Dakota border); Lewis and Clark Pass (in Montana); Lewiston (in Idaho); Clarkston (in Washington State).

men and Native Americans during the whole expedition. After this, Lewis continued eastward, recovering one of the pirogues from a cache and exploring the Marias River before proceeding down the Missouri. Shortly before reaching the meeting point, he had a hunting accident and was shot in the hip.

Clark's group had a less eventful trip and was the first to arrive at the meeting point. During the first week of August, the two groups made contact again, and the reunited Corps of Discovery started the final stage of its journey.

A triumphant return

In mid-August the Discoverers made a return visit to the Mandan villages. Charbonneau and another man took their leave of the corps. The rest of the group, accompanied by a Mandan chief, continued downriver.

As they traveled down the Missouri, the explorers met trappers and traders who gave them news of the outside world. Among the things they learned was that they were believed to have perished, no news of them having reached the United States for more than a year. Finally, on September 23, 1806, nearly two and a half years after they had set out, the surviving members of the Corps of Discovery arrived back at St. Louis where they received a "hearty welcome."

The Achievements of Lewis and Clark

The journey of Lewis and Clark was in itself a great achievement. For one year, five months, and 24 days, the explorers traveled, often where no white people had been before, toward their goal—the Pacific Ocean. After resting for the winter, they made the return trip in just six months. For the United States, the expedition was a bold move that confirmed the ownership of its newest possession—the Louisiana Territory—and a claim to the Oregon region. For Lewis and Clark, the success of the expedition was a tribute to their qualities of leadership.

Despite all the hazards that they faced—mosquitoes, grizzly bears, snakebites, white-water rapids, and diseases caused by poor diet—the expedition suffered no serious casualties, and all but one returned safely. The sad exception to this was Sergeant Floyd, who died from illness shortly after the expedition first set out. He was buried by the side of the Missouri River (see map on page 18).

An extract from the expedition's journal for September 19, 1805, while the corps was still in the foothills of the Rocky Mountains.

our rout lay along the ridge of a high mountain course S 20. W.- 18. me used the snow for cooking. -
Thursday September 19th 1805.
Set out this morning a little after sunrise and continued our rout about the same course of yesterday or S. 20. W. for 6 miles when the ridge terminated and me to our inexprofable joy discovered a large tract of Prairie country lying to the S. W. and widening as it appeared to extend to the W. through that plain the. Indian informed us that the columbia river, (in which we were in search) ran. this place appeared to be about 60 miles distant, but our guide assured us that we should reach its borders tomorro the appearance of this country, our only hope for subsistance greatly, revived the sperits of the party already reduced and much weakend for the want of food. - the country is thickly covered with a very

The journals

Perhaps the greatest achievement of the journey was the thoroughness with which Lewis and Clark followed President Jefferson's instructions. During the course of the expedition, whatever hardships they were suffering, Lewis and Clark kept detailed daily journals. In them they recorded everything that they saw, and made thousands of scientific observations and measurements. At the time, these journals provided a wealth of valuable information for the American government, scientists, and potential settlers. Today, the journals of Lewis and Clark provide fascinating insights into the America of nearly 200 years ago.

In only one sense was the expedition a failure. Lewis and Clark did not find a practical river route to the Pacific Ocean. No such river route existed, and the expedition traveled along rivers that

A Day on the River

The following is based on Lewis and Clark's journal entry for Monday May 13, 1805, when the expedition was making slow progress:

Course	Distance traveled	Notes
35° SW	1½ miles	Two tributaries enter from right—one 60 feet wide, the other 100 feet wide.
50° SW	1 mile	Cliff on the right
75° NW	2 miles	Woodland on left
80° SW	2½ miles	Camped near woods

Total distance traveled today 7 miles

White explorers and Native Americans meet in peace. Lewis (with hand raised) still wears his official uniform. Clark and the others are wearing Native American clothing.

were often impractical for normal boats and crews to use. Ordinary traders could not make such a journey. However, in terms of geographical knowledge, the expedition was a great success. The journals recorded every bend in every river, and each change of direction was measured by compass.

Spreading the word

Lewis and Clark had been given particular instructions about the Native Americans that they would meet. These people were to be informed that the territory in which they lived now belonged to the United States and that they were entitled to live peacefully under the protection of the United States government. The word *peacefully* was to be emphasized. Instead of going to war, any disputes were to be referred to the U.S. government for settlement. If any of the Native American chiefs wished to visit the U.S. government, Lewis and Clark were instructed to make suitable arrangements.

In order to emphasize the authority of the American government, many of the gifts distributed by Lewis and Clark contained symbolic messages. The most important chiefs were given American flags and encouraged to fly these flags from poles in their camps and villages. Other chiefs were presented embroidered uniform jackets of the type worn by officers in the United States Army. The third type of "official" gift was a series of commemorative

A Pawnee chief pictured in 1821. Around his neck he is wearing a medal like the ones presented by Lewis and Clark.

medals of silver, some of which bore a portrait of President Jefferson. By giving these official gifts, Lewis and Clark were doing two things. They were showing their respect for the authority of the chiefs while at the same time proclaiming the distant authority of the American government.

Nature and science

The members of the Corps of Discovery were fortunate to travel through territory that had not yet been changed much by human hands. Most of the Native Americans were not farmers, so little land had been cleared for crops. Almost the only permanent marks made by the Native Americans on the landscape were some ceremonial mounds, and a few rock drawings on riverside cliffs. The Corps of Discovery saw America as nature had created it, before it was transformed by settlers.

Wildlife abounded almost everywhere the expedition went. Large herds of elk and buffalo roamed on the prairies, deer filled the woods, and beavers lived along the rivers. At first, many of the species that the explorers came across were familiar to them. However, as Lewis and Clark moved farther

Beavers on the bank of the Missouri River. According to Clark, the best part of the beaver to eat was the tail.

Bighorn sheep in the Rocky Mountains

A page from Clark's journal with his description and drawing of a white salmon trout (silver salmon)

Lewis's woodpecker, named after its discoverer

west, they found more and more unfamiliar species, and Lewis's scientific training was put to good use.

Sometimes a discovery was made by accident, for example, when one of the expedition shot a deer or bird, only to find that it was a new, unknown species. At other times, tracking down a new species was more difficult. Lewis and Clark had seen the curled horns of a bighorn sheep preserved as a trophy in a Native American lodge long before they saw one of these animals in the wild. Prairie dogs also proved elusive. Lewis wondered for several days about the small holes he saw in the prairie before he caught sight of one of these burrowing animals.

Whenever a new species was discovered, Lewis made a careful description of it in his journal. He recorded its measurements and described its appearance and color. Whenever possible, specimens of birds and small animals were stuffed and preserved and stored in underground caches, to be taken back to the United States for further study. Both expedition leaders gave their names to plant and animal species that they discovered, for example, Lewis's woodpecker and the ragged robin plant *Clarkia pulchella*.

Native Americans

The journals also contain fascinating information about the Native Americans that the expedition came across. Details of dress, ornaments, weapons, and dwellings were all carefully recorded. The Yankton Sioux, for example, lived in cone-shaped tepees made from buffalo skins draped over a lightweight framework of poles. Easily taken down and transported, these tepees were well suited to the Yankton's wandering life-style when they were on a hunting expedition. Farther north, the Mandan had a more settled existence. They lived in round huts made of logs and covered with earth. On the slopes of the Rocky Mountains, the Nez Percé built rectangular lodges, and covered the sides and roofs with woven grass matting. The largest of the Nez Percé lodges measured over 95 feet long and was inhabited by more than 100 people.

The Mandan lived in round huts made of logs and covered with earth.

Most Native Americans used tools made from stone, wood, or animal bone. Metal tools were a rarity, and were usually obtained from white traders. Among the Shoshone, for example, Lewis and Clark noted only a few metal knives, some battered brass kettles, and some metal arrowheads. Others made do with even less. One Native American that they met had a tool kit containing only a few sharp pieces of rock and a length of bone.

Although each tribe had its own traditions and ceremonies, some customs were shared by many Native Americans. Smoking a pipe of tobacco and passing the pipe from person to person was a symbol of peace and friendship. Many white people also enjoyed tobacco smoking by this time, so the members of the expedition found no difficulty in joining in. Some of the tribes grew their own tobacco, while others obtained theirs by trade.

Both explorers and Native Americans had interpreters, so communication was fairly easy. Once they realized that the expedition posed no serious threat, the chiefs were usually pleased to answer the explorers' questions. The explorers' skill with medicines was appreciated, and the expedition occasionally traded medical treatment for food and clothing.

Besides curing minor ailments and injuries, Lewis and Clark were also interested in the general health of the Native American population. Were their numbers increasing or decreasing?

Many of the Native Americans that Lewis and Clark met claimed to be survivors of groups that had once been much larger. During the journey, the explorers also saw many signs of abandoned villages. Questioning revealed that most of the tribes had suffered from outbreaks of smallpox within the previous 50 years. Smallpox was a European disease that had been

A Native American chief smoking a pipe of peace. This photograph was probably taken toward the end of the 19th century.

introduced into America by the first settlers and explorers. Because Native Americans had no natural resistance to this disease, each outbreak of smallpox meant a large number of deaths. Smallpox and other European diseases, such as measles, greatly reduced the number of Native Americans during the 17th to 19th centuries. Although Lewis and Clark noted the effects of smallpox on the Native Americans that they met, they did not realize the full extent of the problem.

Survival in the wild

The success of the expedition showed that a well-organized party of white people could survive in the interior of North America. Most of the time it was possible to live off the land by hunting deer, buffalo, and birds. The rivers also provided abundant food—catfish in the Missouri and salmon in the Columbia. When wild food was scarce, the expedition was able to trade for food with the Native Americans. Had they not been traveling, the explorers would have been able to build up their own food supplies in order to survive the winter.

Although they preferred to live off the animals that they shot, Lewis and Clark also paid close attention to what the Native Americans ate. They noted several species of wild plants that had edible parts, for example, the chestnut-flavored roots of the flowering plant Western Spring Beauty, and the root of the wild turnip plant. Such "wilderness foods" formed an important part of the diet of many Native Americans and were later used by white settlers as survival foods.

Native North Americans

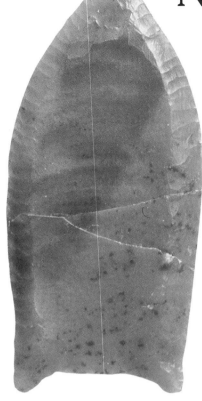

This spearhead is about 10,000 years old. It was used for hunting by the early inhabitants of North America.

When Columbus first landed on the islands of the Caribbean in 1492, he was convinced that he was close to India. When he came across the native people, he called them "Los Indios"—Indians. Although Columbus was later proved wrong about where he had made landfall, his name for the people stuck. The name "Indian" was soon used to describe all the native inhabitants of America. Today, many people prefer the term "Native American."

The first inhabitants of North America were probably people who crossed over the frozen sea from Siberia to Alaska at the end of the last Ice Age. Although the date is uncertain, most of the evidence suggests that these people arrived in North America possibly as early as 30,000 years ago. Spreading south from Alaska, the first Native Americans reached the tip of South America about 10,000 years ago.

No one knows how many Native Americans there were at the time of Columbus. Estimates put the population in North America at that time between one and four million. These Native Americans were divided into hundreds of different tribes. Many of the tribes had their own language, and there were at least 50 different native languages spoken in North America. Some of the tribes were part of larger groups, often known as nations, for example, the Sioux nation. Members of the same nation usually spoke languages that were similar to each other. Sometimes, different tribes would join together to form a league against a common enemy, for example, the tribes of the Iroquois League.

Other Europeans soon followed Columbus. These Europeans made contact with the Native Americans in the Caribbean, and Central and South America, as well as in North America. Often these contacts were disastrous for the Native Americans. Some Native Americans were made slaves. Many died in open conflict with the Europeans, and thousands more died of European diseases. Some Native American groups disappeared completely. Once the Europeans arrived, Native American life changed forever.

Native American groups
The Native Americans living in North America in the early 16th century can be divided into at least six major groups. Scholars have classified these groups according to where the Native Americans lived and their life-styles. These divisions are the following: Eastern Woodlands; Far North; Plains; Northwest Coast; California-Intermountain; and Southwest. The lines of division have never been exact, and different scholars use different systems of classification.

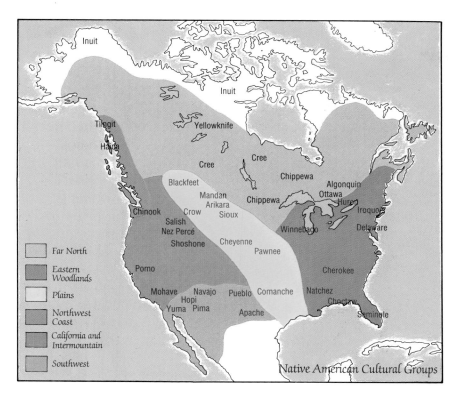

Native American Cultural Groups

Far North

Eastern Woodlands

Plains

Northwest Coast

California and Intermountain

Southwest

Eastern Woodlands

When the English, Dutch, and French began to settle in North America, the people of the Eastern Woodlands occupied the lands stretching from southern Canada to the Gulf of Mexico, and as far west as the Mississippi River. These Native Americans were both hunters and farmers.

The tribes living in the northeastern part of the continent included the Delaware, the Huron, and the Winnebago, among others. But probably the most powerful Native Americans in the Northeast were the Iroquois. The Iroquois organized a group of tribes into the Iroquois League for trade and defense. These Native Americans often took part in the colonial wars on either the British or French side. Among the Native American tribes living in the Southeast were the Cherokee, the Choctaw, the Natchez, and the Seminole.

Far North

The Native Americans of the Far North lived in lands that stretched from eastern Canada as far west as Alaska. Here, the land is covered with dense coniferous forest and dotted with lakes. Among the tribes living in this area were the Algonquin, the Chippewa, the Ottowa, and the Cree. For the most part, these peoples were hunters and gatherers. They wore fur-lined clothes and lived in lodges made of wooden frameworks covered with birch bark or animal hides. In order to travel and hunt during the winter, they often wore snowshoes, and used sledges to drag home their prey.

The Plains

While traveling along the Missouri River, Lewis and Clark encountered several tribes of Native Americans (the Oto, the Yankton Sioux and the Teton Sioux, and the Mandan) who lived on the Plains. Among other tribes living on the Plains

A Mandan chief painted by George Caitlin in 1885.

A buffalo-skin shield made by the Crow tribe. Like other Plains tribes, the Crow used buffalo for food, clothing, and shelter.

were the Cheyenne, the Comanche, the Crow, and the Pawnee.

The vast expanses of plains and prairies stretched from Mexico to Canada, and from the Mississippi River to the Rocky Mountains. This area included almost all of the land in the Louisiana Purchase. Grasslands stretching from horizon to horizon formed the characteristic landscape of this area. Before Europeans arrived in the Americas, the peoples of the Plains had usually lived in villages near rivers and raised crops. In summer they would venture out onto the Plains to hunt buffalo on foot.

The introduction of the horse and gun changed this way of life. Now entire tribes could follow the buffalo on horseback, and killing buffalo became much easier. As a result, many inhabitants of the Plains adopted a nomadic life-style, moving from place to place to hunt buffalo. They used buffalo

Dog to Horse

In South America, early people had domesticated the native llama and guanaco. Besides providing meat and wool, the llama could also be used to transport goods. However, before the arrival of Europeans, there were no suitable animals for domestication in North America. The only animal that Native Americans were able to use was the dog. Small sledges pulled by dogs were used by many North American tribes.

When European settlers arrived, they brought horses with them. Gradually, Native Americans also began to acquire horses. By the beginning of the 19th century, the horse had transformed the way of life of many tribes. Horses allowed some Native Americans to travel farther and faster, and this changed the way that they hunted and made war.

One of the most familiar pictures of Native Americans is that of the warrior on horseback.

But it is important to remember that the horse was unknown to Native Americans until about 1500.

An old photograph showing members of the Cheyenne tribe. The tepee in the background is of a traditional design. The horse, however, was unknown to Native Americans until about 1500. Before then, the travois (sledge) would have been much smaller and pulled by dogs.

Comanche horse-men. The introduction of the horse and the gun changed the way of life of the Plains Native Americans.

Sioux moccasins, made about 1895. They are decorated with beads and dyed porcupine quills.

meat for food and buffalo hide for clothing. They made tools and utensils from buffalo horn and bone, and they used buffalo droppings as a source of fuel.

The first Native Americans encountered by Lewis and Clark, the Missouri, had lived in permanent villages until they were almost completely wiped out by disease and warfare. The last of the Missouri tribe joined the Oto tribe, which is where Lewis and Clark found them. The Oto had some permanent villages, but mostly they followed the buffalo and led a nomadic life.

Lewis and Clark next met the Yankton Sioux and the Teton Sioux, two of the branches of the Sioux nation. Although the Yankton Sioux hunted buffalo, they lived in permanent villages and were farmers, too. The Teton Sioux, however, moved from place to place following the buffalo and living in tepees.

Sign Language

Many different languages were spoken by the North American tribes. These languages developed because of the great size of the continent, which meant that contact between peoples was limited by the distance that they could walk. The introduction of the horse meant that much greater distances could be covered, and contact between tribes increased. On the Plains, where several tribes speaking different languages hunted the same buffalo herds, the Native Americans developed a kind of sign language. By using this sign language, members of different Plains tribes could communicate information and ideas to one another.

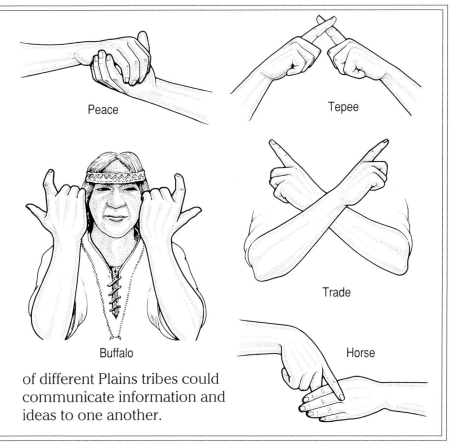

Peace

Tepee

Trade

Buffalo

Horse

Northwest Coast

The Native Americans of the Northwest Coast lived along the Pacific coast from southern Alaska to northern California. Among the tribes in this area were the Chinook, the Haida, and the Tlingit.

The forests, rivers, and ocean all provided abundant food for these Native Americans. The peoples of the Northwest made most of their tools from wood, bone, and shell. They built their homes of wood and carved designs on their doorposts. After obtaining iron tools from white people, the Native Americans made more tall, carved totem poles out of tree trunks.

The tribes that lived on the coast hunted seals and sea otters for their valuable fur. To do this, they built large seagoing canoes that were up to 65 feet in length. The ends of these canoes were often carved into images of birds and animals.

California and Intermountain

This group of Native Americans lived throughout California and extended into the Rocky Mountains. Among the tribes in this group were the Salish, the Mohave, the Nez Percé, the Shoshone, and the Pomo.

In California, people lived mostly in small villages. They ate a

A mask made by the Haida people who lived on the Northwest Coast.

Many members of the Navajo tribe still make their traditional textiles in the Southwest.

Horizons

You could find out about the following objects, which all formed part of Native American life: tomahawk (small ax); coup stick (for touching an enemy without killing him); moccasins (soft leather shoes); buckskin (deer hide); jerky (dried strips of meat); pemmican (preserved meat and berries); travois (a type of sledge); wampum (beads sometimes used as money); adobe (sun-dried bricks).

diet of wild plants and small animals. In the mountainous region, life was more difficult, and the tribes did not settle but stayed on the move. When horses arrived, the Shoshone expanded their hunting grounds and became buffalo hunters.

Although the people of this group probably had the most primitive way of life of all the Native Americans, they were skilled craftspeople and artists. The baskets produced by the Pomo tribe are generally considered to be some of the most beautiful ever made anywhere in the world.

Southwest

The Native Americans of the Southwest lived on lands that now make up the southwestern part of the United States and northern Mexico. Some of the Southwest tribes, such as the Hopi, lived in permanent villages with irrigated fields. Other tribes, such as the Pima and the Yuma, had a less settled existence. The better-known tribes in the Southwest, the Apache and the Navajo, were relative newcomers to the area. They migrated south from Canada around A.D. 1000. Today, their descendants are the most numerous of all Native Americans.

What Happened Later

Personal histories

In November 1804, Thomas Jefferson was elected to serve a second term as President of the United States. In 1809, he retired from politics and devoted his energies to establishing the University of Virginia. He died on July 4, 1826, the 50th anniversary of the signing of the Declaration of Independence, which he had helped to write. Today, he is remembered as one of the Founding Fathers of the United States, and for the purchase of the Louisiana Territory.

Following the success of his expedition, Meriwether Lewis seemed to have a promising career ahead of him. In 1807, he was appointed governor of the Louisiana Territory. For two years he worked hard to bring order to this wilderness. However, in the summer of 1809, he became ill, and on October 11 of the same year, Lewis either was killed or committed suicide.

William Clark fared much better. At first he was put in charge of Indian affairs for the Louisiana Territory, and he became an expert on Native Americans. He later served as governor of the Missouri Territory. He died on September 1, 1838. His servant, York, was given his freedom some time after the expedition.

Toussaint Charbonneau continued to live among the Mandan for another 30 years. Sacagawea moved away from white settlements and probably died in 1812.

National expansion

The United States continued to expand its territory during the 19th century. In 1819, the United States acquired Florida from Spain. The whole eastern side of the continent, from Maine to the Caribbean, was now under American control. In 1836, Texas won its independence from Mexico through an armed struggle that included the famous Battle of the Alamo. In 1845, the Republic of Texas became the 28th state of the United States.

In 1846, a dispute between the United States and Britain over the Oregon Country was finally settled when the two countries signed a treaty. The treaty established the western boundary of the United States with Canada along the 49th parallel (49° north latitude). The land south of the parallel became American territory. In 1848, the United States defeated Mexico in a war and acquired California and all Mexican land north of the Rio Grande River. The United States was now a transcontinental power, stretching from the Atlantic Ocean to the Pacific Ocean.

Although America was united politically, there were deep conflicts within the nation. A bitter dispute over slavery divided the country. In the 1850s, this dispute broke out into open warfare in the Kansas Territory, part of the Louisiana Purchase

Ironclad ships were used for the first time in the Civil War.

area. In 1861, several southern states, following the example of South Carolina, broke away from the United States. Civil war began between the northern states (or Union) and the southern states (or Confederacy). Arkansas and Louisiana, two more states created from the Louisiana Territory, joined the Confederacy in 1861.

The Civil War was the first truly modern war, and machine guns, ironclad ships, and submarines were all used for the first time. The war lasted until 1865 when the North finally defeated the South. After the Civil War, the U.S. continued its territorial expansion, purchasing Alaska from Russia in 1867, and acquiring Hawaii in 1898.

Exploring the West

Other expeditions into the western reaches of the United States followed close on the heels of Lewis and Clark. A scientific expedition sponsored by the United States government explored the Red River in Oklahoma and Texas in 1804-05. During 1805-06, an army officer named Zebulon Pike led an expedition along the upper reaches of the Mississippi River. But Pike is more famous for his exploration of the Southwest in 1806-07. On that trip he traveled through Colorado and New Mexico. In the foothills of the Rocky Mountains, he saw a distant, snowcapped mountain, which was too far away to climb. This peak was later named Pike's Peak.

Slowly but surely, settlers began to move beyond the

Mississippi. In the early 1820s, the Santa Fe Trail from Missouri to New Mexico was opened up so that trade could be developed with the Southwest. In 1824, James Bridger, a fur trader and explorer, journeyed to the Great Salt Lake in present-day Utah. Other American explorers, such as Jedediah Smith and John C. Frémont, found routes through the Rocky Mountains. Now the way to Oregon was open, and wave after wave of

The explorers James Bridger (above) and John C. Frémont (right)

Panning for gold. The gold rush in 1849 saw thousands of people traveling west.

settlers moved west from Missouri along the Oregon Trail.

The discovery of gold at Sutter's Mill in California in 1848 tempted even more people to travel west. The great gold rush of 1849 saw thousands of people flooding west by any means possible. By the end of the year, the population of California had increased from about 27,000 to an estimated 100,000 people.

Slowly, the lands of the Louisiana Territory were settled. The first state from the territory to become part of the United States was Louisiana in 1812. It was followed by Missouri in 1821 and Arkansas in 1836. Eventually, 13 other states or parts of states would be made up of lands that were once part of the territory. In 1907, Oklahoma became the last Louisiana Territory state admitted to the United States.

Machines played a large part in the development of the American West. After the Civil War, guns became widely available. The most famous of these was the revolver pistol, designed by Samuel Colt. This gun could fire six shots without reloading. By 1870, many people west of the Mississippi carried a gun, and disputes were often settled by violence.

During the 1880s, railroads were extended right across America, making it possible to travel from the Atlantic to the Pacific Ocean by train. Settlers who wanted to go west no longer

Sutter's Mill in California where the first gold was discovered.

The Slaughter of the Buffalo

The large number of guns carried by people in the West had a devastating effect on the wildlife there. Wild animals soon became scarce in many areas, but the most alarming effect was on the Plains buffalo.

In 1800, there were at least 50 million buffalo living on the prairies and Great Plains. By 1900, the species was nearly extinct, with only a few hundred animals remaining. Although Native American tribes hunted the buffalo, most of the damage was done by white hunters. Some white hunters made the train journey westward just to kill buffalo. One hunter alone accounted for over 4,000 animals in just 17 months, an average of eight buffalo every day!

Since the beginning of the 20th century, the American buffalo has been a protected species, and it is now no longer in danger of extinction.

White hunters hunted the buffalo almost to extinction.

had to make the trip by wagon. Instead, they could travel in the comfort of a train that ran on a regular schedule. Among some Native Americans, the steam locomotives that pulled the trains became known as "iron horses."

The "Trail of Tears"

As the United States grew, the situation of the Native Americans became worse. The 19th century was a century of misery and destruction for most Native Americans. In the early 1800s, the

The forced march of Native Americans to new lands set aside for them and depicted in the Trail of Tears (a 20th-century painting shown above) was a much different version of the route to the West from the one portrayed by the idealized painting (shown on the right) of settlers traveling in covered wagon trains.

United States government forcefully removed groups of Native Americans from the southeastern part of the United States and relocated them on lands west of the Mississippi River. The name the "Trail of Tears" was given to the long marches of the Cherokee, the Choctaw, the Creek, the Chickasaw, and the Seminole to the new "Indian Territory" in what is now Oklahoma. Thousands of Native Americans died on these forced journeys.

The Native Americans living in the vast lands of the Louisiana Territory also suffered. As the number of white settlers increased in the West, so did the number of conflicts between the settlers and the Native Americans. Periodic warfare throughout the latter part of the 19th century slowly reduced the number of Sioux, Comanche, Kiowa, and other Plains dwellers.

The United States government sometimes tried to deal fairly with the Native Americans, making treaties with them and acknowledging their rights over certain lands. But the treaties were often broken, and Native Americans were forced to live on lands specially set aside for them, called reservations. Even Oklahoma, which had been called "Indian Territory," was opened to settlers and once again the Native Americans lost their land.

During their struggles with whites, the Native Americans had some notable leaders. Among these were Sitting Bull and Crazy Horse of the Sioux, Chief Joseph of the Nez Percé, and Geronimo of the Apache.

An Arapaho robe from about 1920. The robe depicts a battle between U.S. government soldiers and Native Americans on horseback.

American explorers

Meriwether Lewis and William Clark were two brave and resourceful young men who carried out their instructions and treated everyone they met with humanity and respect. Although they helped to open up the American West by their explorations, they share none of the blame for the tragedy that later befell the native population and wildlife of the region. Their journey stands as a proud achievement, untouched by later history.

The same courageous spirit of exploration and adventure that took Lewis and Clark across the Louisiana Territory was repeated by other explorers, such as Robert Peary and Matthew Henson to the North Pole, and Henry Morton Stanley to find David Livingstone in East Africa. Eventually it would take Americans to the moon.

Sitting Bull (left) and Geronimo (below) were among the most outstanding Native American leaders in the long struggle against white people.

Horizons

You could find out about the following people and organizations that all played a part in the history of the American West: Davy Crockett (politician and pioneer); William F. Cody (Buffalo Bill, hunter and showman); William Bonney (Billy the Kid, an outlaw); Wyatt Earp (a lawman); Wells, Fargo & Company (a stagecoach service); Pony Express (a postal service); the U.S. Cavalry (especially the 9th Cavalry, made up of African Americans).